Navigating the Life Enrichment Model™

Take Control of Your Life and Your Circumstances

Workbook and Coaching Guide

Ervin (Earl) Cobb

Charlotte D. Grant-Cobb, PhD

Copyright © 2010 by Richer Life, LLC

Published by RICHER Press
An Imprint of Richer Life, LLC

2320 East Baseline Road, Suite 148-214, Phoenix, Arizona 85042
www.richerlifellc.com

Cover Design: Richer Media USA

No part of this publication may be reproduced, stored in a retrieval system, or transmitted in any form   or by any   means, electronic, mechanical, photocopying,   recording,   scanning, or otherwise, except as permitted under Section 107 or 108 of the 1976 United States Copyright Act, without prior written permission of the publisher.

Library of Congress Cataloging-in-Publications Data

Navigating the Life Enrichment Model™
Ervin (Earl) Cobb and Charlotte D. Grant-Cobb
p.   cm.

1. Psychology   2. Relationships   3. Reference
ISBN 978-0-9744617-4-8 (pbk : alk. Paper)

ISBN 13: 978-0-9744617-2-4

PRINTED IN THE UNITED STATES OF AMERICA

First edition

CONTENTS

How to Use This Guide

We are delighted that the *Life Enrichment Continuum™* evolved as a consequence of our focused use of deductive reasoning, our research of relevant topics and the hundreds of hours of collaboration with colleagues and friends. We are convinced that this innovative paradigm, as embodied within the *Life Enrichment Model™*, can provide the *additional insight*, *broader perspective* and *enhanced focus* we all require in order to diligently approach the life altering events and circumstances we encounter in our lives. The *Life Enrichment Continuum™* is summarized in Part Three of this guide (pages 43-45).

Use this Guide to apply the *Life Enrichment Model™* to major events and the resulting circumstances that you may encounter in your life. We recommend, prior to starting this project, that you read the book which accompanies this guide --- *Living a Richer Life: Getting the Most out of Life's Gifts and Circumstances.*

You should carefully follow the directions as set forth within each section.

You should not attempt to complete this project in one sitting. You should give yourself time to thoughtfully complete each section. It would be helpful to involve others, i.e. family members, friends, a professional coach or someone you trust, to be a part of what should be a confidential evaluation, analysis and course of action. Honest feedback from others can be extremely helpful in order to gain a more complete and healthier perspective of your circumstance.

You should give your project a name, i.e. *Project Make It Happen*. This will help to remind you that it also needs your attention as you go about other important daily tasks.

Your goal is to clearly and thoroughly understand your situation, your options and the potential consequences of your action or inaction. You should think through all the circumstances and potential opportunities that may be available to shape a more positive outcome.

Remember to consider all of your personal, professional and spiritual gifts as well as other resources that can be brought to bear to this situation. You should properly address all of the circumstances you are facing as a result of the event. Be mindful of what it will take to seize the potential opportunities and whether or not you are up to the task at this time.

Be diligent about planning the tasks and activities required to generate the desired outcomes. You must follow through on what must be done. Give this project the focus and priority it deserves. By starting and completing this project, we are sure you will make better decisions, feel better about the outcomes and experience the addition of richness in your life.

If we can be of any assistance with individualized, one-on-one coaching [via email, teleconference or in person], do not hesitate to contact us. There may also be opportunities for you to attend a local presentation or a group workshop in your area.

You can find information on RICHER LIFE presentations and workshops at www.richerlifeassociates.com.

We wish you the best as you strive to get the most out of your gifts and circumstances. By doing so, you are on your way to living a richer life.

Part One

THE
LIFE ENRICHMENT
MODEL™

The Life Enrichment Model™

When properly applied, the *Life Enrichment Model™* can become an exceptional tool to aid in identifying unforeseen opportunities and determining the paths available to you as you encounter potentially life altering circumstances. The results of the model's queries can help you get into *the position* [both mentally and practically] to make better decisions, take appropriate actions and to more consciously make the adjustments required to formulate your responses to shape more positive outcomes.

When you provide honest and realistic responses to the model's queries and assumption-capturing techniques, it can become a significant complement to your own natural gifts and your efforts *to live a richer life*.

The Figure 1-1 presents a graphical presentation of the *Life Enrichment Model™*, its five stages and the sequential flow of all of the model components.

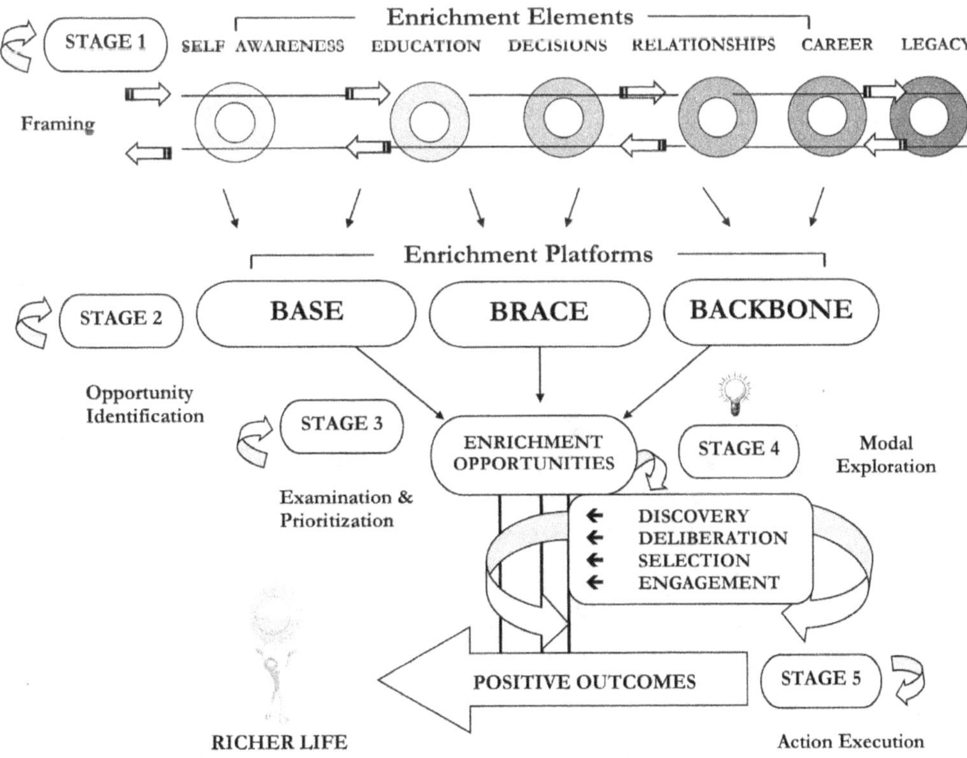

Figure 1-1-Graphical Representation of the Life Enrichment Model™

During certain stages, the *Life Enrichment Model™* constructively provides you figurative depictions and characterizations of the intangibles [such as state of mind, behavioral tendencies and emotional conditions] in your life at the time you encounter a major circumstance. The depictions and characterizations are generalizations and should to be used *as a guide* to steer you in the best direction. When you merge these *generalities* with your own timely [internal and external] observations and sound reasoning, this combination gives you a significant advantage as compared to simply *reacting* and *going it alone*.

The Life Enrichment Model™ Components

This section presents the five stages of the *Life Enrichment Model™* as well as detailed descriptions of each model component and its role in the modeling process.

I.   THE FRAMING STAGE

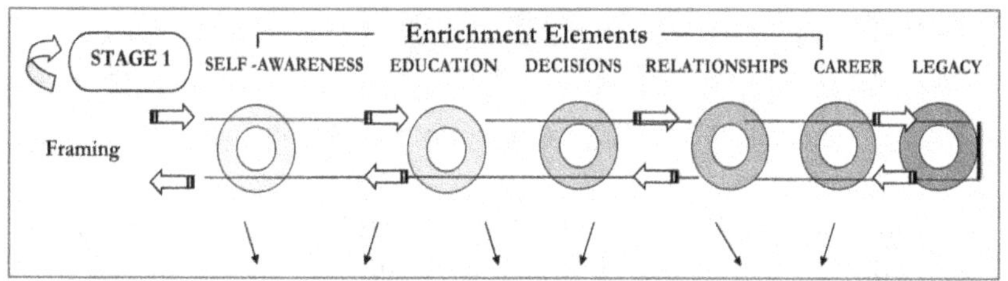

Figure 1-2 – The Framing Process

The **Framing Stage** is the first step in the *Life Enrichment Model™*. In this stage the goal is to extract a view or *frame* of your *mind-set* in order to reveal how you can place yourself in the best position [mentally] to identify and examine opportunities embedded within life altering circumstances. The modeling components used to perform this step are the *Framing Process, Framing Elements* and the *Framing Query*.

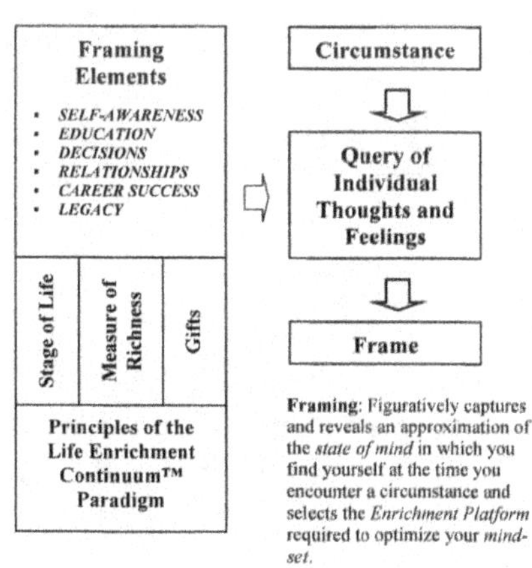

Figure 1-3 - The Framing Process

The Framing Process uses the Framing Query and the Framing Elements to aid in determining the "probable mind-set" present when you first encounter major events. Figure 1-3 details the activity associated with the Framing Process. The output of the Framing Process is an approximation of your *perspective* at that time. It is believed that this *approximation* is consistent with the "probable mind-set" you will take into the encounter. The *mind-set* you take into an encounter can influence what you think, how you think and how you perceive the surrounding circumstances.

The primary focus of the Framing Stage is to ensure that the representation exemplified by the Framing Elements all have a "top-of-mind" position in your perspective prior to moving into the *Opportunity and Identification* Stage of the model. This is achieved by *optimizing* or augmenting your mind-set with the representation set forth by the *Platform Archetypes*.

This optimization allows you to enhance your perception of the situation, craft a more targeted response to the circumstance and shape more positive outcomes. Figure 1-4 outlines the Enrichment Platforms and presents a description of the *Platform Archetypes.*

Enrichment Platform	Structural Focus	Target of Mind-set Optimization	Archetypal Character
BASE	Foundational Elements	Strengthens sense of "who we are" and "what we can learn"	· Awareness Anchor · Education Enthusiast
BRACE	Supportive Elements	Strengthens sense of "what happened along the way" and "why quality and alignment matter"	· Decisions Dynamo · Relationship Rancher
BACKBONE	Core Elements	Strengthens sense of "re-invention is par for the course" and "it comes back ten-fold"	· Career Carver · Legacy Leaver

Figure 1-4 -Enrichment Platforms and Archetypes

The Framing Stage's output is an enhanced *perspective* optimized to obtain a broader and more concise perception of the event being encountered.

II. THE OPPORTUNITY IDENTIFICATION STAGE

The **Opportunity Identification Stage** is the second step in the *Life Enrichment Model™*. In this stage the goal is to develop an initial list of circumstances which appear to have surfaced as a result of the situation at hand. The goal is to evaluate each circumstance to identify embedded opportunities and then analyze each opportunity to determine its potential for life enrichment. This step also involves detailing and documenting the desired outcomes.

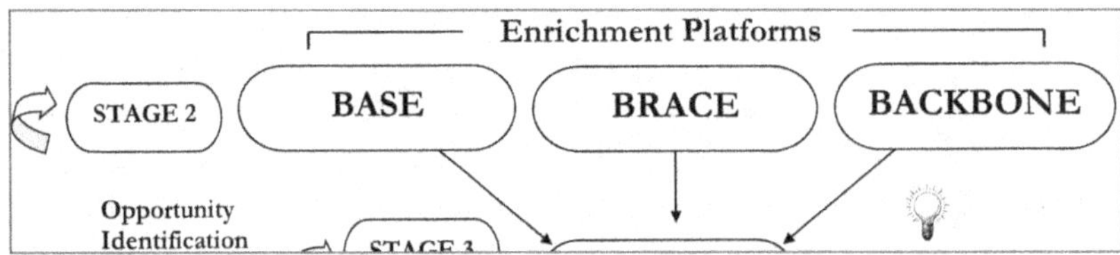

Figure 1-5 - Opportunity Identification

The components used to perform this step are contained in *Step-One* of the TWO-STEP Opportunity Identification Methodology. Figure 1-6 details the activity associated with opportunity identification.

Prior to this Stage, the results of the Framing Query have been used to identify the Enrichment Platform that is required to launch the Opportunity Identification Stage [See Figure 1-5]. From the Enrichment Platform you gain sufficient exposure to the representations and insights embodied within the *Platform Archetype.*

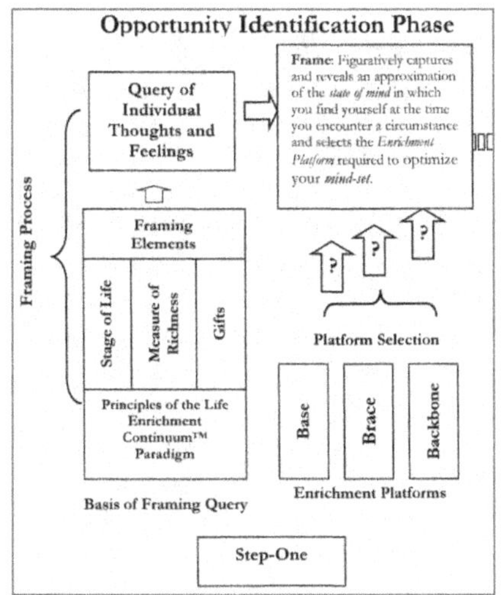

The objective is to ensure that the characterizations represented by the Framing Elements all have a "top-of-mind" position in your theater of thought as you establish your initial perception of the event.

The output of the Opportunity Identification Stage is a list of circumstances, embedded opportunities and desired outcomes associated with the event.

Figure 1-6 – Opportunity Identification

III. THE EXAMINATION AND PRIORITIZATION STAGE

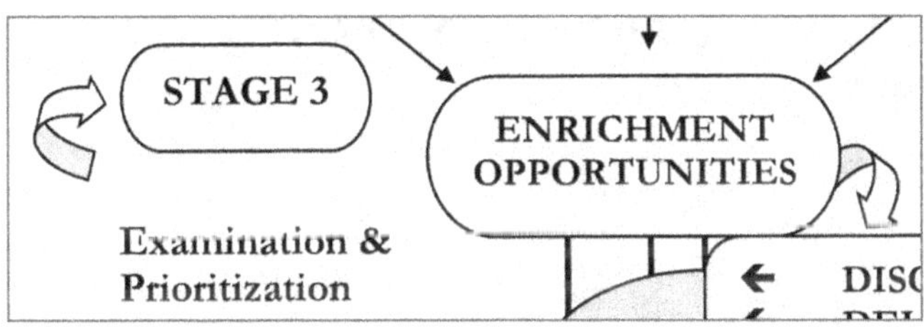

Figure 1-7 - Examination and Prioritization

The **Examination and Prioritization Stage** is the third step in the *Life Enrichment Model™*. In this stage the goal is to take the list of circumstances and associated opportunities generated within the Opportunity Identification Stage and decide which opportunities have the highest probability to enrich your life. The selected opportunities must also be within your reach and your ability to realize them at this time.

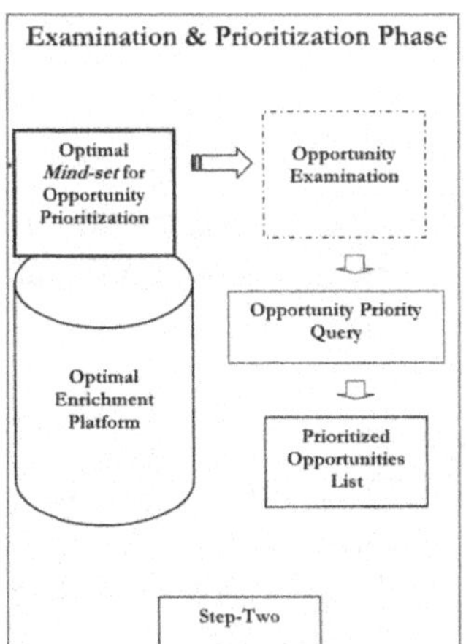

The modeling components used to perform this step of the process is *Step-Two* of the Two-Step Opportunity Identification Methodology and a stimulating set of questions developed to focus your thoughts during opportunity prioritization, called the *Priority Query*. Figure 1-8 details the activity associated with the Opportunity Identification Phase. The *Priority Query* in presented in Figure 1-9.

Figure 1-8 - TWO-STEP Methodology

The actual prioritization is determined by your responses to the *Priority Query.* The Examination and Prioritization Stage's output is a list of *actionable opportunities* which are believed to have the potential to shape a more positive outcome to the event at hand.

This set of circumstances and *actionable opportunities* becomes the focus of the last two stages of the model, **Enrichment Examination** and **Action Execution.**

Opportunity Priority Query

1. *Do I have the physical, psychological & intellectual strength and stamina to take on what is required to move this situation, from where it is today, to where I envision it has to be, in order to obtain the value & richness I perceive it will add to my life, when fully realized?*

2. *Do I have or can I acquire the level of resources [financial, moral & spiritual] required to seize the opportunity?*

3. *If I decide to do nothing, am I ready to accept and live with the consequences that may arise as a result of this circumstance?*

Figure 1-9 - Opportunity Priority Query

IV. THE ENRICHMENT EXAMINATION STAGE
(Modal Exploration)

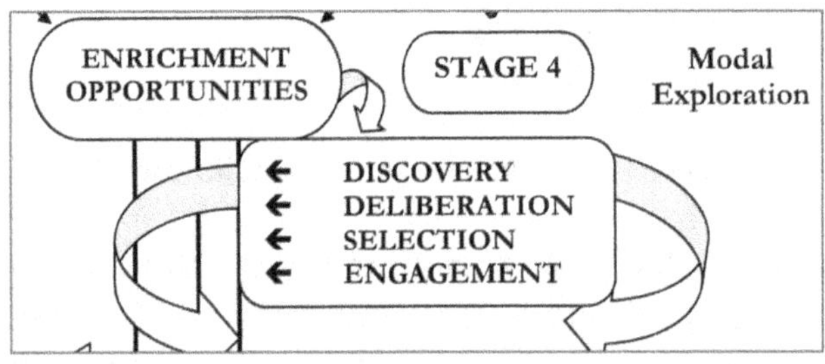

Figure 1-10 - The Modal Exploration Stage

The **Enrichment Examination Stage** is the fourth step in the *Life Enrichment Model™.* In this stage the goal is to sequentially and systematically examine more intensely each set of circumstances and *actionable opportunities* identified in the Examination and Prioritization Stage.

This intense examination uses a process called *Modal Exploration.* The Modal Exploration process is both thought provoking and methodical. With potential Enrichment Opportunities as its input, it utilizes a series of custom designed inquiries to lead you through a guided exploration of each circumstance. The output of a successful exploration is the completion of the actions as documented during the engagement mode. Figure 1-11 summarizes the objectives and outcomes of each the four modes involved in the Modal Exploration Process.

The Enrichment Examination Stage culminates in the *Selection Mode.* In the Selection Mode you must decide to either *engage* in moving forward with the planning and execution of the tasks associated with *seizing* the enrichment opportunity or decide to not respond to the circumstance at hand in this fashion. A decision not to pursue the opportunity concludes the exploration.

Exploration Mode	Activity and Objectives
Discovery	• In the **Discovery Mode** the objective is to develop a concise summary and description of each circumstance surrounding the *event* or *situation* at hand. This activity is fueled by a thoughtful and thorough examination of all aspects of the situation. • This Mode also generates a concise set of statements that describe the opportunities available to you [at this time] in order to shape a more positive *outcome*, *result* and *future*, as a consequence of *the event* and *your response.*
Deliberation	• The **Deliberation Mode** involves the attainment of a detailed understanding of the opportunity and the documentation of *what will be required of you and others* in order to seize the opportunity.
Selection	• In the **Selection Mode** you must make a decision to either *pursue the opportunity* or to *respond to the circumstance* with another approach. • A decision NOT to pursue this *particular* opportunity concludes this exploration.
Engagement	• In the **Engagement Mode** you will develop and execute the *action plan* required to seize the opportunity. This mode also contains the follow-up activity required to determine the actual outcome and its impact on your life's richness.

Figure 1-11 - Modal Exploration

Part Two

THE LIFE ENRICHMENT MODEL™
Application Guide

APPLICATION GUIDE

Project Name_______________________________ **Date Started**______________________________

1.0 The Framing Stage

Goal:	To extract a view or *frame* of your mind-set in order to reveal how you can place yourself in the best position to identify and examine opportunities embedded within a circumstance.
Input:	Review of the five stages of the Life Enrichment Model™ and detail descriptions of each model component to become familiar with their role in the modeling process.
Output:	An approximation of your current *perspective*. It is believed that this *approximation* is consistent with the "probable mind-set" you will take into your evaluation of the event and circumstance at hand.
Model Components:	*Framing Process, Framing Elements* and the *"Framing Query"*.

Application Steps:

1. Summarize your thoughts regarding your current view or perspective of the situation at hand.

2. Complete Framing Query (See "Framing Query" Reference Sheet - Page 53).

3. Grade your Framing Query results to determine Enrichment Platform (See "Grading the Framing Query" Reference Sheet – Page 57).

4. Examine the Archetypes associated with the Enrichment Platform as determined by the Framing Query results (See "Platform Archetypes" Reference Sheets -Page 71).

5. Evaluate the thoughts you recorded in step 1 now that you have reviewed the Platform Archetype and note how your perspective of the situation may have changed at this point.

6. Move to the next stage, The Opportunity Identification Stage.

Summary of my view and perspective of the situation at hand.

Changes in my perspective regarding the situation after the Framing Archetype review.

APPLICATION GUIDE

2.0 The Opportunity Identification Stage

Goal:	Evaluate each circumstance to identify embedded potential opportunities. Then analyze each potential opportunity to detail and document the desired outcomes.
Input:	A sufficient exposure to the characterizations and insights embodied within the *Platform Archetype* suggested by the Framing Query results. This will aid in ensuring that all characterizations represented by the Framing Elements all have a "top-of-mind" position.
Output:	A list of circumstances, embedded opportunities and desired outcomes associated with the situation you are facing along with the insight and awareness gained through the evaluation and analysis process.
Model Components:	Step-One of the TWO-STEP Opportunity Identification Methodology.

Application Steps:

1. Develop a list of circumstances, embedded opportunities and desired outcomes.

2. List ALL circumstances you perceive as apparent. Be specific and detail each opportunity and each desired outcome. Each circumstance should be unique but may be related to other circumstances.

3. Move to the next stage, The Examination and Prioritization Stage.

Opportunity Identification

List of Circumstances	Potential Opportunities	Desired Outcomes
1.	1. 2. 3.	1. 2. 3.
2.	1. 2. 3.	1. 2. 3.
3.	1. 2. 3.	1. 2. 3.
4.	1. 2. 3.	1. 2. 3.

APPLICATION GUIDE

3.0 The Examination and Prioritization Stage

Goal:	To take the list of circumstances surrounding the situation at hand and decide which opportunities have the highest probability to enrich your life and are consistent with your capability to realize them at this time.
Input:	The list of "potential opportunities" developed during the Opportunity Identification Stage.
Output:	A list of the most actionable opportunities.
Model Components:	TWO-STEP Opportunity Identification Methodology and *Opportunity Priority Query.*

Application Steps:

1. For each opportunity on your list, respond to each question of the Opportunity Priority Query. (See "Opportunity Priority Query" Reference Sheet – Page 49)

2. Based on your response, select the most actionable opportunities which may shape a more positive outcome to the situation at hand.

3. Move to the next stage, The Modal Exploration Stage.

Examination and Prioritization

Opportunity	Opportunity Priority Query Question #1		Opportunity Priority Query Question #2		Opportunity Priority Query Question #3		Actionable Opportunity ?
1.	YES	NO	YES	NO	YES	NO	YES ☐ NO ☐
2.	YES	NO	YES	NO	YES	NO	YES ☐ NO ☐
3.	YES	NO	YES	NO	YES	NO	YES ☐ NO ☐
4.	YES	NO	YES	NO	YES	NO	YES ☐ NO ☐
5.	YES	NO	YES	NO	YES	NO	YES ☐ NO ☐
6.	YES	NO	YES	NO	YES	NO	YES ☐ NO ☐
7.	YES	NO	YES	NO	YES	NO	YES ☐ NO ☐
8.	YES	NO	YES	NO	YES	NO	YES ☐ NO ☐
9.	YES	NO	YES	NO	YES	NO	YES ☐ NO ☐
10.	YES	NO	YES	NO	YES	NO	YES ☐ NO ☐
11.	YES	NO	YES	NO	YES	NO	YES ☐ NO ☐
12.	YES	NO	YES	NO	YES	NO	YES ☐ NO ☐

APPLICATION GUIDE

4.0 The Modal Exploration Stage

Goal:	Examine the list of most "actionable opportunities" to decide to either respond to the circumstance by pursuing the opportunity or to respond to the circumstance with another approach.
Input:	List of actionable opportunities from the Examination and Prioritization Stage.
Output:	An action plan for seizing each opportunity to be pursued. NOTE: A decision not to pursue the opportunity concludes the exploration process.
Model Components:	Modal Exploration process.

Application Steps:

1. Examine the list of actionable opportunities using the Modal Exploration Process (See "Modal Exploration Process" Reference Sheet – Page 61)

2. During the "Selection" mode of the process decide to either pursue the opportunity or not.

3. In the "Engagement" mode develop an action plan which will generate the desired outcomes.

4. Move to the next stage, The Action Execution Stage.

Modal Exploration Summary

Actionable Opportunity	Exploration Mode	Objectives and Outcomes
1.	Discovery	
	Deliberation	
	Selection	
	Engagement	
2.	Discovery	
	Deliberation	
	Selection	
	Engagement	
3.	Discovery	
	Deliberation	
	Selection	
	Engagement	

APPLICATION GUIDE

5.0 The Action Execution Stage

Goal:	The Action Execution Stage tracks the execution of the actions developed and planned as a part of the Engagement Mode within the Modal Exploration Process.
Input:	Action Plan from Engagement Mode within the Modal Exploration Process.
Output:	Successful execution of actions required to address each circumstance and obtain the desired outcomes.
Model Components:	Engagement Mode within the Modal Exploration Process.

Application Steps

1. Closely track the execution of all actions.

2. Note any follow-up actions that may be required.

THE LIFE ENRICHMENT MODEL™

Action Execution Tracking

Action Item	Action Plan	Date Complete	Follow-up Actions
1.	• What: • Who: • Where: • When: • Desired Result: • Actual Result:		
2.	• What: • Who: • Where: • When: • Desired Result: • Actual Result:		

Action Execution Tracking

Action Item	Action Plan	Date Complete	Follow-up Actions
3.	• What: • Who: • Where: • When: • Desired Result: • Actual Result:		
4.	• What: • Who: • Where: • When: • Desired Result: • Actual Result:		

Part Three

THE LIFE ENRICHMENT MODEL™
Reference Sheets

The Life Enrichment Continuum™

The *Life Enrichment Continuum™* is a paradigm that provides a systematic approach to characterizing [in a practical manner] the various environmental and human behavioral factors that come into play when any of us encounter circumstances in life.

The *Life Enrichment Continuum™* is summarized in terms of its four basic *Enrichment Principles* and corresponding *Enrichment Challenges.* Each Enrichment Principle sets forth a thought provoking observation regarding the environment and the forces at play when you find yourself in the position in life where you must encounter a potentially life changing circumstance. Integrating the Enrichment Principles into your thoughts during these times assists in establishing the *state of mind* optimum to properly identifying embedded enrichment opportunities. The corresponding Enrichment Challenges constitute the knowledge-based objective or target you should attempt to achieve as you shape your responses to the circumstances which surround each event. Collectively, the Principles and Challenges establish the framework required to move you into position to get the most out of life's gifts and circumstances.

ENRICHMENT PRINCIPLE No. 1 - As we travel along the continuum of life, from one stage to the next, we accumulate insights and experiences which alter how we perceive ourselves, how we perceive others and how we respond to opportunities for life enrichment.

ENRICHMENT CHALLENGE No. 1 - *To recognize life enrichment opportunities presented to us as we travel along the continuum of life and to leverage the experience, maturity and wisdom we have accumulated by shaping our behaviors, perceptions and responses in order to take advantage of these opportunities.*

ENRICHMENT PRINCIPLE No. 2 - Negative outcomes as a result of encountering a circumstance, at any time along the continuum of life, can and most often impede life enrichment. Positive outcomes have both near and long term impacts and, in most cases, significantly enhance the richness [quality, fullness and abundance] in our lives.

ENRICHMENT CHALLENGE No. 2 - *To leverage the refinement and growth of our humanistic gifts (qualities) as we travel along the continuum of life in order to facilitate as many positive outcomes and eliminate as many negative outcomes as possible.*

ENRICHMENT PRINCIPLE No. 3 – The measure of richness in our life is based on the societal norms of the day and is an omnipre   43   erception which significantly influences our behaviors and responses to life's challenges   ircumstances.

ENRICHMENT CHALLENGE No. 3 - *To maintain an awareness and perspective of the norms that are in vogue [such as fashionable, trendy, modish] within society and to establish our own individual measure and perception of richness in our life as we respond to life's challenges and circumstances.*

ENRICHMENT PRINCIPLE No. 4 – Positive outcomes which result from taking advantage of enrichment opportunities later in life may have the potential of significantly offsetting the impact of negative outcomes at earlier stages in our life.

ENRICHMENT CHALLENGE No. 4 - *To enrich our lives to the fullest, we must not only recognize enrichment opportunities embedded within life changing circumstances but we must also take the actions necessary to ensure that we fully realize [gain the full impact of] as many positive outcomes as possible.*

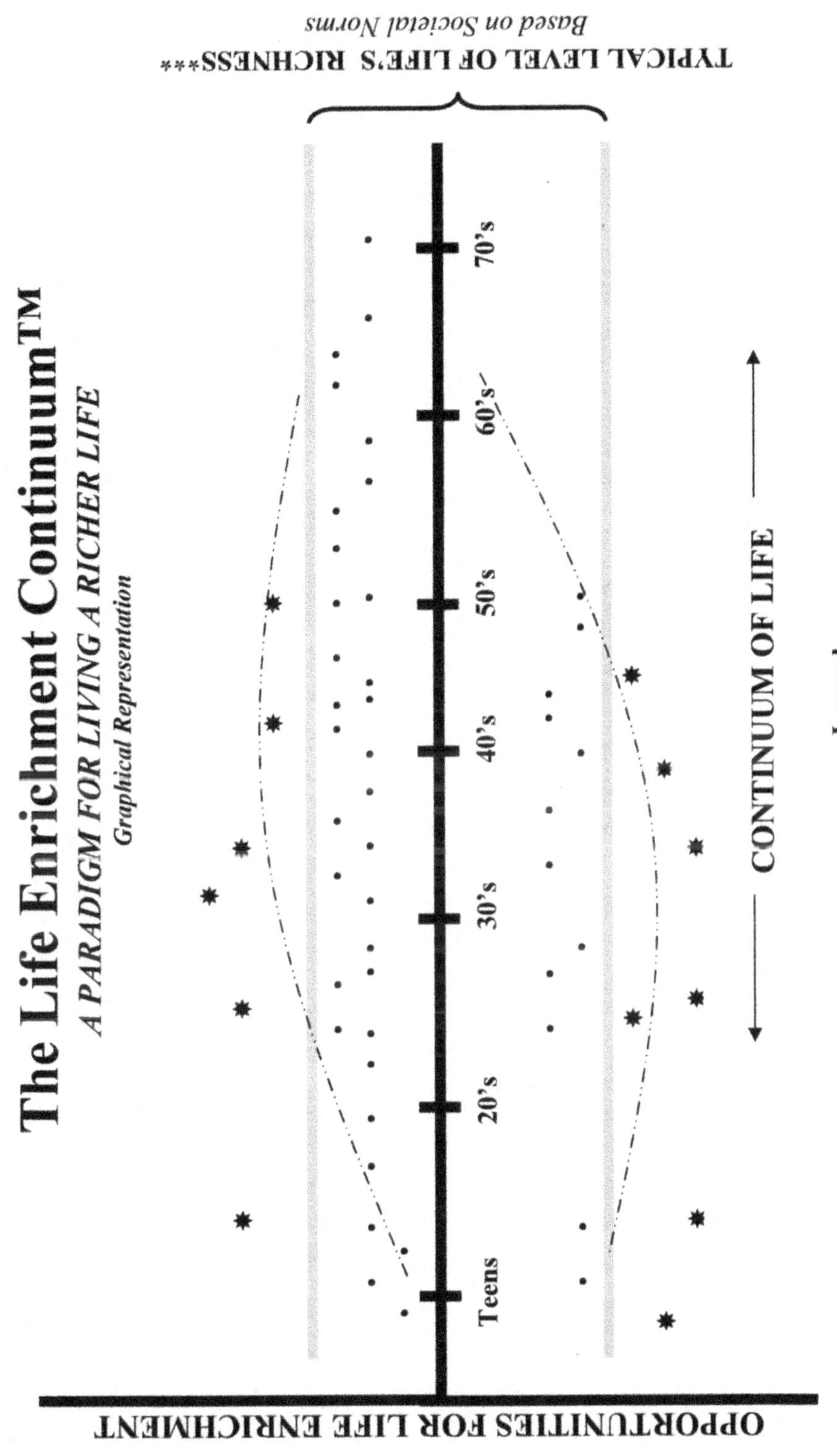

——————————————— Legend ———————————————

Opportunities for Life Enrichment along the Continuum of Life - *embedded in circumstances as a result of major life events.*

Outcomes to Circumstances which Change One's Life from Status Quo – *either enhancing or impeding life's richness.*

Perception of the Richness of One's Life - *based on societal norms and shaped by individual actions or in-actions in response to inevitable circumstances in life.*

***RICHER LIFE:\'rich\\'lif\ - *a life full of good decisions, financial security, great relationships, loving family memories and a feeling of completeness.*

The Framing Process

The *Framing Process* systematically approximates your mind-set at the time you face a major circumstance. The school of thought and general thesis of the *Framing* methodology is as follows:

Our state of mind and perspective can be generally characterized by capturing an *inventory of your thoughts* surrounding six structural components, referred to as *Framing Elements*. These *Elements* are believed to comprise an underlying system or structure that gives shape, strengthens and frames *who you are* and *what you think* at the time you initially encounter a major circumstance in your life.

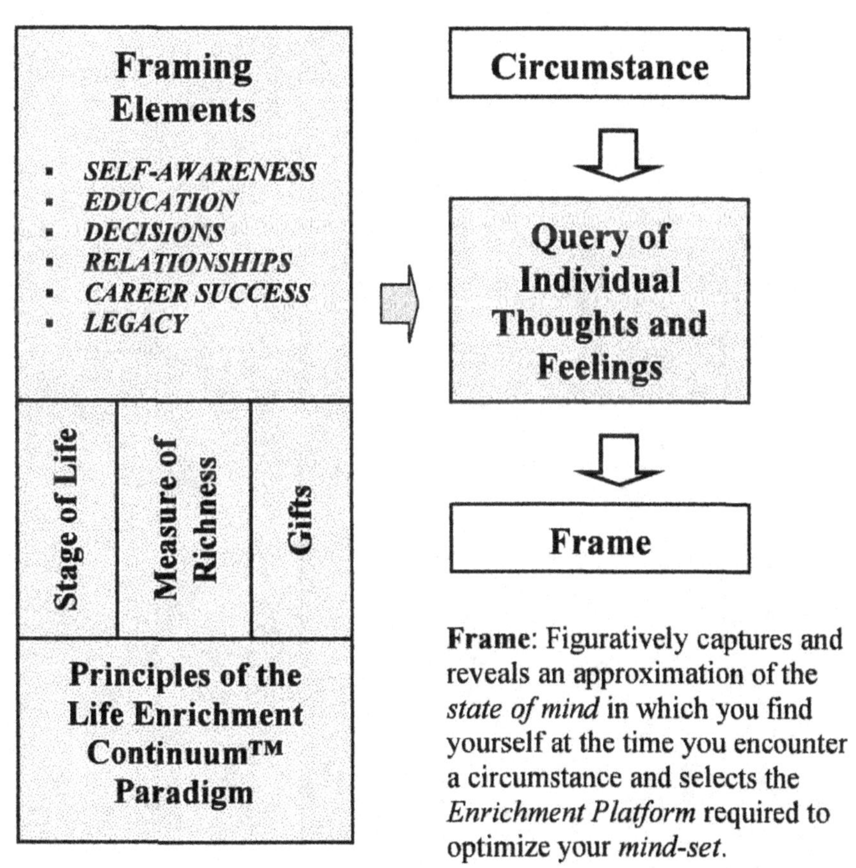

Frame: Figuratively captures and reveals an approximation of the *state of mind* in which you find yourself at the time you encounter a circumstance and selects the *Enrichment Platform* required to optimize your *mind-set*.

The Opportunity Priority Query

1. *Do I have the physical, psychological & intellectual strength and stamina to take on what is required to move this situation, from where it is today, to where I envision it has to be, in order to obtain the value & richness I perceive it will add to my life, when fully realized?*

	YES
	NO

If No: Why Not? What are your concerns?

2. Do I have or can I acquire the level of resources [financial, moral & spiritual] required to seize the opportunity?

	YES
	NO

If No: Why Not? What are your concerns?

3. *If I decide to do nothing, am I ready to accept and live with the consequences that may arise as a result of this circumstance?*

	YES
	NO

If *No: Why Not? What are your concerns?*

The Framing Query

Provide the "Best Answer" to each question below by responding with either True (T) or False (F)

Questions	Response (Circle one)	
1. Being self-aware allows me to recognize my emotions and their effects on my life.	True	False
2. Self-awareness limits my ability to accept candid feedback.	True	False
3. Even with a high level of self-awareness it is difficult to be confident about a situation when there are uncertainties and pressures involved.	True	False
4. Being self-aware means knowing more about others and how they view me.	True	False
5. A lower level of self-awareness makes it easier for others to understand me.	True	False
6. Having an accurate sense of who I am helps me decide what areas in my life I should improve.	True	False
7. Self-awareness helps to know my strengths but not cope with my weaknesses.	True	False
8. My emotional self-awareness makes me a more effective and intuitive decision maker.	True	False
9. Education is the knowledge of putting our potentials to maximum use.	True	False
10. It is not possible to be a life-long learner as you get older.	True	False
11. Learning is best done in the classroom.	True	False
12. There is more to good education than just demonstrating reading, writing, listening and speaking skills.	True	False
13. Even with an education, it still may not be possible to understand and remember new information.	True	False
14. I find it easy to adapt new methods to move forward.	True	False
15. I have obtained all of the education I need to be successful in life.	True	False
16. Life long learners are generally college educators with multiple degrees.	True	False
17. Generally, options are limited in most circumstances.	True	False
18. When options are limited I make decisions quickly since things most likely will not change.	True	False
19. I should always make a list of every possible outcome to all major circumstances I encounter.	True	False
20. I should never trust my intuition when making a difficult decision.	True	False
21. If I am not gifted in an area of competence that will help me make a better decision, I will make a good guess instead of bothering someone that I trust.	True	False
22. When it is difficult to choose between two options, I most often choose the one that is supported by both logic and intuition.	True	False

23. I should not focus on drawing insight and wisdom from every decision I make.	True	False
24. I do not have to feel comfortable with a decision if it is the correct one.	True	False
25. There are many qualities that make up positive and valuable relationships.	True	False
26. Because most relationships are so complex, you have to accept what you get.	True	False
27. I should always attempt to grow, leverage and maintain positive, valuable relationships.	True	False
28. My interpersonal skills are important but not critical to a good relationship	True	False
29. I should concern myself with the impact of my decisions only if they involve family members and close friends.	True	False
30. Knowing too much about others makes it difficult to grow a quality and positive relationship since there is little to learn and discover.	True	False
31. A good relationship does not have any give-and-take when it comes to tackling challenging circumstances.	True	False
32. I should take full responsibility for learning as much about the other person as possible.	True	False
33. I am only partially responsible for my career because I will always need help from others.	True	False
34. Having a successful career is not one of the most important factors in achieving my life goals.	True	False
35. In order to keep my career on track, I must continuously update my skills and knowledge.	True	False
36. Your current job or position is never the best place to start from when you are trying to move your career forward.	True	False
37. If required, I have the power and determination to re-invent my career.	True	False
38. A network of colleagues and acquaintances is good, but not a necessary part of managing my career and finding the best opportunities for advancement.	True	False
39. You should always be prepared for the next opportunity.	True	False
40. A successful career will be free of all negatives and disappointments.	True	False
41. My overall success in life will define the future success of my legacy.	True	False
42. There are only a few good reasons for valuing and leaving a legacy.	True	False
43. Most people do not require some kind of assistance from others.	True	False
44. To leave a legacy I simply need to give a gift to a charity.	True	False
45. If I give to private foundations, I lose all personal control of who gets my help.	True	False

46. Community foundations only accept large cash donations.	True	False
47. A community foundation can pool funds and achieve economies of scale for investing, managing and granting philanthropic dollars.	True	False
48. The act of giving itself reinforces who we are as human beings.	True	False

Grading the Framing Query and Selecting Archetypes

Step# [1] Place your responses in Column #2			Step# [2]	Step# [3]	Step# [4]	Step# [5]
Question #	Your Response (T or F)	Answer Key	Place an "X" next to the answers which match the Answer Key.	Total the number of "X's" for each of the three groups and place total in Box	Rank from 1 to 3 the "Totals" from Step #3 (With "1" being the highest total and "3" the lowest total).	Thoroughly review the Archetypes below associated with the LOWEST RANKED Group in Step # 4. This will optimize your *mind-set* prior to moving to the Opportunity Identification Stage.
1		T				
2		F				
3		F				
4		F			(If you have a" TIE ", review all Archetypes)	
5		F				
6		T				**Platform: BASE**
7		F				*Platform Archetypes*
8		T		[ ]	( )	**Awareness Anchor**
9		T				and
10		F				**Education Enthusiast**
11		F		TOTAL	Group A RANK	
12		T				
13		F				
14		T				
15		F				
16		F				
17		F				
18		F				
19		T				
20		F				
21		T				**Platform: BRACE**
22		T				*Platform Archetypes*
23		T				**Decisions Dynamo**
24		F		[ ]	( )	and
25		T				**Relationship Rancher**
26		F			Group B	
27		T		TOTAL	RANK	
28		F				
29		F				
30		F				
31		F				
32		T				

Grading the Framing Query and Selecting Archetypes
(Continued)

Step# [1] Place your responses in Column #2			Step# [2]	Step# [3]	Step# [4]	Step# [5]
Question #	Your Response (T or F)	Answer Key	Place an "X" next to the answers which match the Answer Key.	Total the number of "X's" for each of the three groups and place total in Box	Rank from 1 to 3 the "Totals" from Step #3 (With "1" being the highest total and "3" the lowest total).	Thoroughly review the Archetypes below associated with the LOWEST RANKED Group in Step # 4. This will optimize your *mind-set* prior to moving to the Opportunity Identification Stage.
33		F				
34		F				
35		T				
36		F				
37		T				**Platform: BASE**
38		F				*Platform Archetypes*
39		T				**Career Carver**
40		F	[ ]	( )		and
41		T				**Legacy Leaver**
42		F			Group C	
43		F	TOTAL	RANK		
44		F				
45		F				
46		F				
47		T				
48		T				

The Two-Step Opportunity Identification Methodology

      The TWO-STEP Opportunity Identification Methodology guides your thought process as you examine and prioritize opportunities and shape your responses to the circumstances. The methodology is designed to identify the most favorable starting point or optimal *platform* for entering into the opportunity examination process.

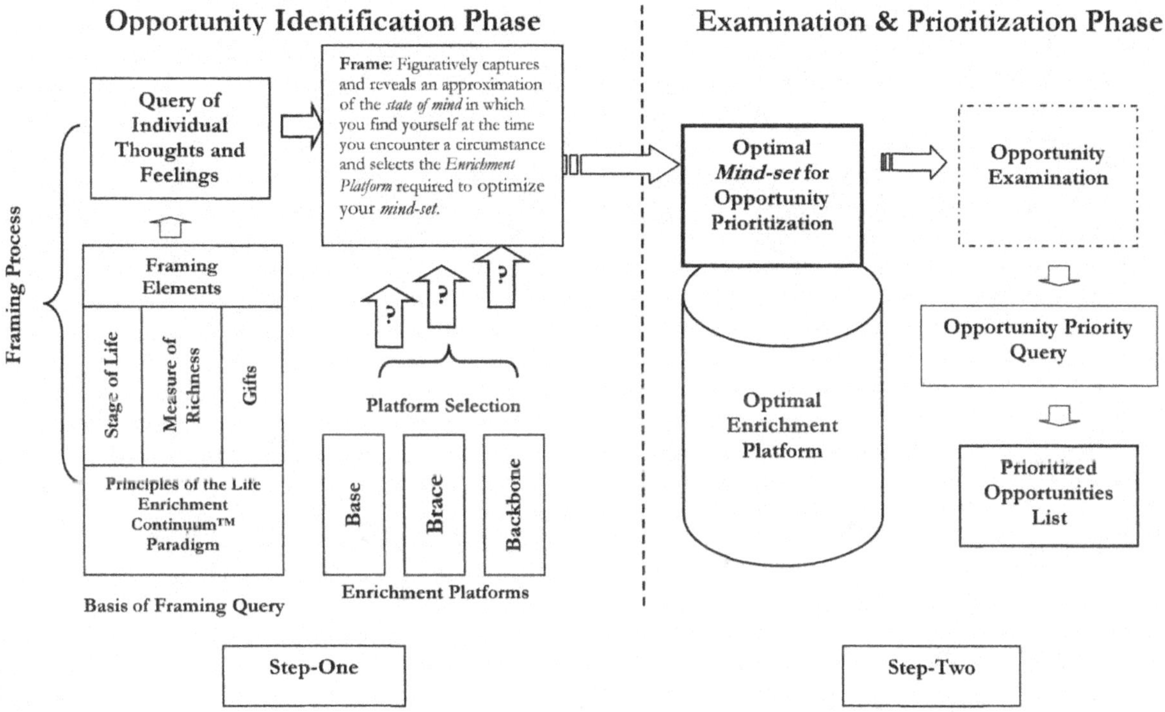

The Modal Exploration Process

Exploration Mode	Activity and Objectives
Discovery	• In the **Discovery Mode** the objective is to develop a concise summary and description of each circumstance surrounding the *event* or *situation* at hand. This activity is fueled by a thoughtful and thorough examination of all aspects of the situation. • This Mode also generates a concise set of statements that describe the opportunities available to you [at this time] in order to shape a more positive *outcome*, *result* and *future*, as a consequence of *the event* and *your response*.
Deliberation	• The **Deliberation Mode** involves the attainment of a detailed understanding of the opportunity and the documentation of *what will be required of you and others* in order to seize the opportunity.
Selection	• In the **Selection Mode** you must make a decision to either *pursue the opportunity* or to *respond to the circumstance* with another approach. • A decision NOT to pursue this *particular* opportunity concludes this exploration.
Engagement	• In the **Engagement Mode** you will develop and execute the *action plan* required to seize the opportunity. This mode also contains the follow-up activity required to determine the actual outcome and its impact on your life's richness.

1.0 Discovery Mode

The circumstance(s) surrounding the event or situation are:

I can best describe the opportunity as follows:

2.0 Deliberation Mode

Summarize the tasks and activities that would be required to seize the opportunity and ensure the desired outcome.

I will need to do the following:

I need to get the following people involved for the reasons noted:

My concerns are as follows:

3.0 Selection Mode

Document the Pros and Cons associated with your ability to complete the tasks and activities required to seize the opportunity. After carefully weighing the Pros, Cons and your ability to execute what is required, then make a decision to either pursue the opportunity or to respond to the circumstance with another approach. A decision not to pursue the opportunity concludes the Modal Exploration process.

The Pros in this situation are as follows:

The Cons in this situation are as follows:

My Concerns with being able to do what is required to seize the opportunity are:

My Decision is:

Basis of my Decision is as follows:

4.0 Engagement and Action Execution Modes

Action	Responsibility	Date Started	Date Completed
1.			
2.			
3.			
4.			
5.			
6.			
7.			
8.			
9.			

Part Four

THE LIFE ENRICHMENT MODEL™
Platform Archetypes

Enrichment Platform: **BASE**
Enrichment Element: **SELF-AWARENESS**

ARCHETYPE
AWARENESS ANCHOR

I am the *Awareness Anchor*. I am emotionally aware. I clearly recognize my emotions and their effects. I know which emotions I feel and why. I recognize how my feelings affect my performance. I have a guiding awareness of my values and goals. I know my strengths and limits.

I am aware of my strengths and weaknesses. I am reflective. I learn from my experiences. I am open to candid feedback, new perspectives, continuous learning, and self-development. I am able to show a sense of humor and perspective about myself.

I am self-confident. I am sure about my self-worth and capabilities. I present myself with self-assurance. I have "presence". I can voice views that are unpopular and go out on a limb for what is right. I am decisive. I am able to make sound decisions despite uncertainties and pressures.

I know that an essential factor in maintaining genuine personal connections with others is through my self-awareness. Through my self-awareness I have the ability to perceive what is going on with me at all times. Since skill of understanding who we are is not taught in school, achieving my level of self-awareness is an extremely difficult assignment.

I became the Awareness Anchor and learned the skill of becoming self-aware through a high level of focus and observation. However, it was my strong desire to attract and cultivate authentic, meaningful and satisfying personal relationships in my life that sustained the effort required to truly know myself.

Over the years, I have learned that the more I understand myself, the easier it is for others to understand me. This has set the stage for more meaningful, rewarding relationships in my life.

Having an accurate sense of who I am helps me decide what areas of my life I can improve. I am able to produce high quality decisions by knowing my strengths and how to cope with my weaknesses. I am not hesitant to consult colleagues and subordinates that I trust to both gain a broader perspective and understand unique details.

My emotional self-awareness allows me to become a more effective and intuitive decision maker. I am able to read my "gut feelings" and use this to help guide timely decisions when facing difficult circumstances. I know who I am at this moment. I am the *Awareness Anchor*.

Platform Archetypes

Enrichment Platform: **BASE**
Enrichment Element: **EDUCATION**

ARCHETYPE
EDUCATION ENTHUSIAST

I am the *Education Enthusiast*. I am aware of the demands of the global workplace. I know the needs of society are changing rapidly. I believe that education, being the knowledge of putting our potentials to maximum use, is key to a productive lifestyle in the 21st century.

I believe that education is more than collecting knowledge without understanding its value. I believe that the processing of knowledge fuels inspiration, visionary ambitions, creativity, motivation and my ability to bounce back from failure. I believe that we all gain true value of knowledge through life-long learning.

I am a life-long learner. I use my strong reading, writing, listening and speaking skills to achieve my life goals. I possess an awareness of what I need to learn and know. I leverage my education and desire to learn to succeed in life by managing day-to-day circumstances. I have worked hard to become interdependent and interpersonally competent. I believe in persistence and responsibility.

It is in my nature to be venturesome and creative. I set specific goals for myself. I understand the value of adopting powerful strategies for attaining my goals. I closely monitor my performance for signs of progress. I am sensitive to the need to sometime restructure my physical and social environment to make it compatible with my goals. I efficiently manage my time. I find it easy to adapt new methods to move forward and build valuable relationships.

I know that it is important to be skilled in identifying, retrieving, and organizing information. I am capable of understanding and remembering new information. I proactively demonstrate critical thinking skills and my ability to reflect on my own understanding. I am self-directed. I am self-regulated. I am self-motivated. I am reflective.

I understand the value associated with being curious and motivated. I recognize the significance of being methodical and disciplined. I realize the power of being logical and analytical. Yet, I know the importance of being self-aware and flexible. When I come face-to-face with difficult circumstances, I carefully assess the situation and ask --- What can I learn?

I am the *Education Enthusiast*.

Platform Archetypes

Enrichment Platform: **BRACE**
Enrichment Element: **DECISIONS**

ARCHETYPE
DECISIONS DYNAMO

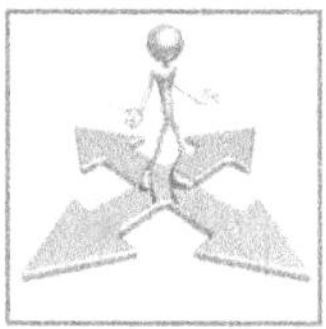

I am the Decisions Dynamo. On my way to making good decisions I always list my options. It may appear that there is only one course of action, but I know that this is usually not true. Even if my situation seems limited, I always manage to identify alternatives.

I always weigh the possible outcomes to every major circumstance in my life. For every possible course of action, I list all possible outcomes. I then label them as either having a positive or negative impact on the richness of my life. One method I use to track this analysis is to place a plus sign (+) next to each positive outcome and a minus sign (-) next to each negative outcome.

I always consult my gift of intuition. If I am not gifted in an area which would help make a better decision, I will always seek input from someone I trust.

I must feel comfortable with all of the decisions I make. I will always make a decision and choose the best option available. I remind myself that making a final decision is always a difficult task. Thus, I focus first on the decisions on my list that are supported by both logic and intuition. My final choice always has more plus signs than negative signs and is always confirmed by my intuition.

I always monitor and evaluate the results and outcomes of my decisions. However, if I do not evaluate my decisions afterward, I will not learn anything from the experience. I need to know whether the outcome was what I expected. I need to know whether or not I would respond to the circumstance in the same way in the future.

In addition, I need to understand what I learned from each encounter with each circumstance.

As the Decisions Dynamo, I consistently focus on drawing insight and wisdom from every decision I make. My goal is always to ensure that every choice has a positive outcome.

Through my self-awareness, I know that regardless of my efforts, I may experience negative outcomes. However, I strive to always be aware of *what happened along the way.*

I am the *Decisions Dynamo.*

Enrichment Platform: **BRACE**
Enrichment Element: **RELATIONSHIPS**

ARCHETYPE
RELATIONSHIP RANCHER

 I am the *Relationship Rancher*. There are many qualities that make up positive and valuable relationships. Good support, compromise and honest communication are just a few of the qualities I desire in all of my relationships. I believe in creating value in my life and contributing value to others.

My definition of value in a relationship includes the ability to grow, leverage and mutually benefit from the association. It also includes a balance between the ups and downs while expecting significantly more positives than negatives. I have learned that in order to grow, leverage and maintain positive, valuable relationships, I must first focus on developing my own relationship skills.

Strong relationship skills allow me to manage and always be in control of what I bring and what I take away from all my relationships. Over time, I have learned that what works best for me are strong communications, interpersonal, decision making and learning skills.

To sharpen my communications skills I speak so that others can understand me. That way, they do not have to guess what's important in my life and what I expect from a particular relationship. I listen actively so that I am sure I understand what's being shared and what's being asked of me. I strive for continuous improvement of my interpersonal skills.

I understand that I must cooperate with others and treat them in the same manner that I wish to be treated. I have found that I must work harder on improving my interpersonal skills as I advance in age and wisdom. I take the time to clearly understand how my decisions will impact others. I am well aware of the need to give in order to receive. I am also mindful of the fact that all relationships are not equal. Sometimes the giving is to support one relationship and the value is returned by means of a different relationship.

I take full responsibility for learning as much about the other person as possible. The more I know about what each of us bring into a relationship the better I will be able to manage and control the unforeseen. I was taught early in life to really know someone, *make sure you are around for all four seasons.* Each of my relationships has its three P's ---Place, Purpose and Position --- in my life.

In any relationship, there is going to be give-and-take as situations and circumstances change. Thus, I make sure that all my relationships are quality relationships. I make sure that they all are properly aligned with the richness I desire in my life. I am the *Relationship Ranger*.

Platform Archetypes

Enrichment Platform: **BACKBONE**
Enrichment Element: **CAREER SUCCESS**

ARCHETYPE
CAREER CARVER

I am the *Career Carver*. I know that in America today, more than ever, I am responsible for building my career and guiding it to the level of success that complements the richness I desire in my life.

I am a life-long learner. I know that one of the major factors for career success is to never stop learning. I know that my world is constantly changing and that just as in life, career success depends on identifying new ways of doing things. I know that in order to keep my career on track, I must continuously update my skills and knowledge.

I am a good listener. Because I am a good listener, I can learn things quickly and avoid many of the schools of hard knocks. I learn from other's experiences.

I know that my current job or position is the best place to start and move my career in the trajectory that I desire. I know that often very little separates the most successful people from the average person. I know that nothing comes free. I know that the best way to advance my career is to do my current job well and fulfill current responsibilities.

I am constantly building and adding to my network of colleagues and acquaintances. I know that my next career step might arise from my contact network. I spend quality time building new contacts and relationships. I never forget to maintain the relationships I already have.

I know that the best way to obtain valuable information from my network is to provide others with the information they are seeking. I am always prepared for the next opportunity. I maintain a current resume and update it regularly. I know that the next step on my career ladder to success may surface tomorrow.

But above all, when I find myself in a position where I am stalled in my career and my success is in jeopardy, I know that I have the power and determination to re-invent myself. I never lose sight of the fact that as we travel along the continuum of life, we will experience both negatives and positives in all phases of our life, including career success.

It is with this understanding that I know that true success in life is to increase positive outcomes and minimize negative outcomes. I know that, at times, success equals maintaining par for the course. I am the *Career Carver*.

Platform Archetypes

Enrichment Platform: **BACKBONE**
Enrichment Element: **LEGACY**

ARCHETYPE
LEGACY LEAVER

I am the *Legacy Leaver*. I know that the key to success is to always start everything you do with an end in mind. I realize that this simple bit of common sense could really be applied to all aspects of life, including career, family, personal relationships and professional goals.

I believe that to live a life of passion and significance requires making noteworthy strives and achievements. As a legacy leaver, I express my personal values by integrating my charitable, family and financial goals.

I know that my overall success in life will define my legacy. I know that there are many reasons for valuing and leaving a legacy. Each is as important as the next. I see legacy giving as a responsibility owed to my community.

I know that most people require some kind of assistance, whether it's physical, financial or spiritual. I am well aware of local church congregation or food banks supplying meals during a tough time. I have seen how a scholarship has made a dream of college possible.

I have witnessed loved ones and friends receive compassionate care in local hospitals during illness or injury. As I travel along the continuum of life, I am reminded that more must be done to continue positive, humane acts of kindness and to sustain programs for personal enrichment.

I take advantage of a number of ways to be philanthropic. I feel good about living my life well and leaving a legacy.

I give to charitable organizations. My gifts to established charities provide direct support to those organizations such as schools, hospitals, arts and cultural institutions, human service agencies and religious organizations. My gifts to these nonprofit organizations vary in size. I give to private foundations. Private foundations allow me to retain personal control and flexibility over giving programs. My gifts to community foundations can be of any size, from as little as a dollar to thousands -- or millions -- of dollars. By pooling funds, community foundations achieve economies of scale for investing, managing and granting philanthropic dollars.

I know that when I give freely and without any expectations of a return, the act of giving itself reinforces who I am as a human being. I know that what I give unconditionally *will come back to me ten-fold* and will enrich my life. I am the *Legacy Leaver*.

Part Five

THE LIFE ENRICHMENT MODEL™
Glossary of Terms

GLOSSARY OF TERMS

BACKBONE

BACKBONE is the third of the three Enrichment Platforms. It is the most substantial and sturdiest component within the Life Enrichment Model™. BACKBONE is anchored by the two *stabilizing* Enrichment Elements ---CAREER SUCCESS and LEGACY. They are characteristic of a mind-set cognizant of what it takes to achieve the level of financial achievement & self-actualization you desire in life.

BASE

BASE is the first of the three Enrichment Platforms. Base is the most fundamental component within the Life Enrichment Model ™. BASE is anchored by the two *foundational* Enrichment Elements --- SELF-AWARENESS and EDUCATION. These Elements, through Platform Archetypes, aid in focusing your thoughts on "Who am I" and "What can I learn" at the time you initially encounter a major life event. Having these thoughts *top-of-mind* should aid your efforts to capture a complete perspective of the situation, the surrounding circumstances and opportunities to shape a more positive outcome.

BRACE

BRACE is the second of the three Enrichment Platforms. BRACE is anchored by the two *action-oriented* elements --- DECISIONS and RELATIONSHIPS. They are characteristic of a mind-set cognizant of what it takes to strengthen the pursuit of your ultimate life goals and reinforcing prosperous alignments with others.

"CAREER SUCCESS"

"CAREER SUCCESS" is one of the two *stabilizing* Enrichment Elements which serve as anchors within the BACKBONE Enrichment Platform.

CONTINUUM OF LIFE

The Continuum of Life is the human life span viewed as a "continuous opportunity" for personal growth and enrichment. As you travel along the *continuum of life*, you acquire additional gifts, talents and wisdom as well as a deeper *awareness* and a broader *perspective* of yourself, your environment and others around you.

"DECISIONS"

"DECISIONS" is one of the two *action-oriented* Enrichment Elements which serve as anchors within the BRACE Enrichment Platform.

DELIBERATION MODE

The Deliberation Mode is the second mode of the Modal Exploration process. In the Deliberation Mode, you are enlightened by the development of a complete understanding of an enrichment opportunity which you have identified as a potential response to a circumstance at hand. This step of the process is completed by documenting *what will be required of you* and *others* in order to *seize* the opportunity.

DISCOVERY MODE

The Discovery Mode is the first mode of the Modal Exploration process. In the Discovery Mode the objective is to develop a concise summary and description of each circumstance surrounding the *event* or *situation* at hand. This activity is fueled by a thoughtful and thorough examination of all aspects of the situation.

"EDUCATION"

"EDUCATION" is one of the two *foundational* Enrichment Elements which serve as anchors within the BASE Enrichment Platform.

ENGAGEMENT MODE

The Engagement Mode is the fourth and final mode of the Modal Exploration process. In the Engagement Mode, you develop and execute the *action plan* required to seize the enrichment opportunity. While in this mode you will also perform the follow-up activity required to evaluate the actual outcome and its impact on your life's richness.

ENRICHMENT ELEMENTS

Enrichment Elements are core sub-structures that constitute the Enrichment Platform. As an aggregate, the Enrichment Elements influence what we think, how we think and how we perceive the circumstances we encounter.

ENRICHMENT PLATFORMS

Enrichment Platforms constitute the core foundation upon which the Life Enrichment Model™ is positioned. Within the model, the Enrichment Platforms figuratively represent the underlying social and economic structure inherent to the work ethic and dreams of the vast majority of the working populace. Each platform consists of two Enrichment Elements.

Glossary of Terms

EXPLORATION MODES

The Explorations Modes are used to examine the enrichment opportunities which may be embedded within the circumstances that surface as a consequence of Life Events. The four Modes are characterized as the Discovery Mode, the Deliberation Mode, the Selection Mode and the Engagement Mode.

FRAMING

Framing is the act of capturing your state of mind at the time a circumstance is initially encountered.

GREATER GIFTS

Great Gifts are qualities which, as compared to other human gifts, more directly contribute to your ability to put yourself in a position to take the actions which will result in positive outcomes. The *greater gifts* are exemplified by the following traits: *Self-awareness*; *Imagination*, *Conscience* and *Independent Will*.

"LEGACY"

"LEGACY" is one of the two *stabilizing* Enrichment Elements which serve as anchors within the BACKBONE Enrichment Platform.

LIFE ENRICHMENT CONTINUUM™

The Life Enrichment Continuum™ is a paradigm that provides a systematic approach to characterizing the various *environmental*, *societal* and *human behavioral* factors that come into play when you encounter major circumstances in life.

LIFE ENRICHMENT MODEL™

The Life Enrichment Model™ embodies the concepts of the Life Enrichment Continuum™. The model is designed as a deductive and interactive tool to support your personal effort to enhance your ability to more effectively respond to major events and circumstances in your life.

LIFE'S CIRCUMSTANCES

Life's Circumstances can take on many forms and can surface either physically, mentally or emotionally. In general, they are conditions or facts that determine, or must be considered in determining, a *course of action* that must be taken to *respond* to Life Events.

Glossary of Terms

LIFE EVENTS

Life Events are noteworthy happenings that can occur at any time throughout your life span. Most events in life are fairly common. Most result in minor changes in your life and in your lifestyle. However, there are events such as the death of a spouse, a long-term loss of employment, a permanent disability, a chronic illness, an early retirement, a home foreclosure, personal bankruptcy and a teenage pregnancy that can cause significant turmoil and change in your life.

LIFE'S GIFTS

Life's Gifts are the natural talents and qualities you are given at birth i.e. mental, physical, emotional, intellectual and sensual abilities as well as those that you acquire via education, experience and maturation as you travel along the *Continuum of Life*.

MODAL EXPLORATION

Modal Exploration is a systematic process which uses a series of custom designed methodologies, queries and approaches to identify, prioritize and examine circumstances in order to seize embedded opportunities for shaping more positive outcomes.

OUTCOMES

An outcome is what follows after you respond or simply react to a circumstance. *Positive* outcomes tend to significantly enhance the level of richness in your life and have both near-term and long-term impacts. *Negative* outcomes seem to always be accompanied with setbacks and have the potential of impeding your growth and prosperity.

PLATFORM ARCHETYPES

Within the Life Enrichment Model™, Platform Archetypes are standards used to illustrate the essence of qualities set forth by each of the six Enrichment Elements.

"RELATIONSHIPS"

"RELATIONSHIPS" is one of the two *action-oriented* Enrichment Elements which serve as anchors within the BRACE Enrichment Platform.

RICHER LIFE

A RICHER LIFE is a life full of good decisions, financial security, great relationships, loving family memories and a feeling of completeness.

Glossary of Terms

SELECTION MODE

The Selection Mode is the third mode of the Modal Exploration process. In the Selection Mode you must make a decision to either *pursue the opportunity* or to *respond to the circumstance* with another approach. A decision NOT to pursue the opportunity concludes this exploration.

"SELF-AWARENESS"

"SELF-AWARENESS" is one of the two *foundational* Enrichment Elements which serve as anchors within the BASE Enrichment Platform.

THEATER OF THOUGHT

Your *Theater of Thought* at the time you face an unexpected Life Event consist of what you *think* and how you *rationalize* the circumstances that have surfaced as a result of the event's occurrence. . Both, your thoughts and your ability to rationalize can be influenced by what is presently dominating your "top-of-mind" and can significantly contribute to how you initially perceive the situation.

TWO-STEP OPPORTUNITY IDENTIFICATION METHODOLOGY

The TWO-STEP Opportunity Identification Methodology guides your thought process as you examine and prioritize opportunities and shape your responses to circumstances. The methodology is designed to identify the most favorable starting point or optimal Platform for entering into the opportunity examination process.

VECTORED CONSEQUENCE

A Vectored Consequence is the result of applying your perspective to *frame* or *view* a circumstance for the first time. The origin of such a consequence [one with magnitude and direction] takes the form of a set of captivating questions which attempts to illuminate the *difficulty of the challenge* at hand [magnitude] as well as the *course of action* that should be taken [direction] in response to the circumstance.

ABOUT THE AUTHORS

Ervin (Earl) Cobb
Charlotte D. Grant-Cobb, PhD

The Cobbs are widely recognized as two of the nation's *rising-stars* among Self-Improvement, Relationships and Inspiration authors, lecturers and speakers.

The collective seriousness and wit of their work has been described as perfect for "those seeking personal growth, change and life enrichment but not quite ready for Dr. Phil."

Their prior books include *Until I Change, Living a Richer Life: Getting the Most out of Life's Gifts and Circumstances, Pillow Talk Consciousness: Intimate Reflections on America's 100 Most Interesting Thoughts and Suspicions, Focused Leadership: What You Can Do Today to Become a More Effective Leader, Transition, Navigating the Life Enrichment Model™ and God's Goodness and Our Mindfulness.*

They currently reside in Phoenix, Arizona.

NOTES

NOTES

NOTES

NOTES

NOTES

NOTES

NOTES

NOTES

NOTES

NOTES

NOTES

NOTES

NOTES

www.ingramcontent.com/pod-product-compliance
Lightning Source LLC
Chambersburg PA
CBHW080457030726
47592CB00011B/3154